Warring in the Spirit: Power for Everyday Living

Cheryl Colwell

Published by Inspired Fiction Books, 2023.

Table of Contents

My deepest thanks go out to my friend and spiritual counselor, Lois Calderwood, who first taught me how to do spiritual battle in name of Jesus Christ. After more than forty years of struggle, I finally experienced victory!

Praise the powerful name of Jesus who strengthens, comforts, and frees us to walk in new life!

Warring in the Spirit: Power for Everyday Living

Published in the United States by Inspired Fiction Books

ISBN: 978-0-9987505-4-5

Categories: Religion/Christian Living/Spiritual Warfare

CHAPTER ONE
WHY WARFARE?

The first spiritual battle we faced was for our hearts to be turned away from our destructive life toward our Father God. God called and tugged at our hearts until we said yes! Now, we are battling our old ways of thinking by having our minds renewed by the Spirit of Jesus Christ. We are learning His ways for victorious living in the kingdom of God.

THE FATHER, SON, AND HOLY SPIRIT

ARE FIGHTING FOR US

All facets of the war for our salvation are accomplished because of God's great love for us. The Father calls us. Jesus paid the penalty for our sins so we could become children of God. Through His Spirit, we are born again and transformed.

We cooperate with Holy Spirit by resisting evil, declaring God's word, confessing, and asking for His help to fill us and strengthen us. It is the Spirit, not our efforts, who does the miraculous work of transformation in us as we abide in Christ. It can trip us up if we feel it is up to us to "be good." Thank God, He is faithful to complete what He began!

Galatians 3:1-3 Oh, foolish Galatians! Who has cast an evil spell on you? ... Let me ask you this one question: Did you receive the Holy Spirit by obeying the law of Moses? Of course not! You received the Spirit because you believed the message you heard about Christ. How foolish can you be? After starting your new lives in the Spirit, why are you now trying to become perfect by your own human effort? (NLT)

John 15:5 "I am the vine, you are the branches. He who abides in Me, and I in him, bears much fruit; for without Me you can do nothing." (NKJV)

Philippians 2:13 ...for it is God who works in you both to will and to do for His good pleasure. (NKJV)

Philippians 1:6 ...being confident of this very thing, that He who has begun a good work in you will complete it until the day of Jesus Christ; (NKJV)

OUR ENEMIES

On the other side of the battle, we have three enemies: 1) the world and its pressure to conform to its standards, 2) our own cravings and woundedness, and 3) the devil's lies that attempt to destroy us.

The world:

John 15:18-19 "If the world hates you, remember that it hated me first. The world would love you as one of its own if you belonged to it, but you are no longer part of the world. I chose you to come out of the world, so it hates you." (NLT)

The flesh:

Galatians 5:17 For the flesh desires what is contrary to the Spirit, and the Spirit what is contrary to the flesh. They are in conflict with each other, so that you are not (able) to do whatever you want. (NIV)

The devil:

1 Peter 5:8 Be sober, be vigilant; because your adversary the devil walks about like a roaring lion, seeking whom he may devour. (NKJV)

Ephesians 6:12 For our struggle is not against flesh and blood, but against the rulers, against the authorities, against the powers of this dark world and against the spiritual forces of evil in the heavenly realms. (NIV)

These are mighty foes. However, we can be confident of ultimate success because God has empowered us with weapons to battle our enemies as the scriptures attest. Further, no matter which enemy is attacking you, they are all equally defeated by the power of God.

JESUS OVERCAME THE FORCES OF EVIL

Luke 4:18-19 "The Spirit of the Lord is on Me, because He has anointed Me to proclaim good news to the poor. He has sent Me to proclaim freedom for the prisoners and recovery of sight for the blind, to set the oppressed free, to proclaim the year of the Lord's favor." (NIV)

If Jesus set us free and healed us, then why do believers become insnared by defeat and anxiety? Why isn't the body of Christ victorious in the work of preaching, healing the broken, or setting captives free? Because the enemy has many of us sidelined—broken down by the side of the road, nursing our wounds, bound in hopelessness, and trying to use the world's solutions to solve our problems. We are believing the lies of the devil instead of believing the Word of God.

No matter what we *feel* is true, as believers we hold on to what the Word says is true by the power of the Holy Spirit. This is the only way to live in victory—living as Christ did, by the Word of God.

CHAPTER TWO

OUR WEAPONS ARE NOT THE WORLD'S WEAPONS

2 Corinthians 10:3-5 For though we live in the world, we do not wage war as the world does. The weapons we fight with are not the weapons of the world. On the contrary, they have divine power to demolish strongholds. We demolish arguments and every pretension that sets itself up against the knowledge of God, and we take captive every thought to make it obedient to Christ. (NIV)

1. Discernment

When a negative emotion shows up, listen and hear the words that are causing you to feel that way. See if you can identify what you are feeling. Practice discerning the differences between feelings.

1 Corinthians 12: 7, 10 But the manifestation of the Spirit is given to each one for the profit of all: for to one is given the word of wisdom through the Spirit, ...to another the working of miracles, to another prophecy, to another discerning of spirits... (KJV)

Hebrews 5:13-14 For everyone who partakes only of milk is unskilled in the word of righteousness, for he is a babe. But solid food belongs to those who are of full age, that is, those who by reason of use have their senses exercised to discern both good and evil. (NKJV)

Jesus discerned when a spirit was at work in a person, spoke directly to it, and rebuked it. He also knew when someone was being deceived by a lie or needed to receive or give forgiveness. He cautioned us against allowing a root of bitterness to spring up within us, which keeps anger trapped inside. It takes time spent in communion with Holy Spirit and practice to discern which spirit is at work.

It could be:

-an actual demon that is harassing us

-a sin, spirit, or attitude that is entrenched in us, such as a *haughty* spirit

-a lie we are believing about ourselves, about God, or about someone else

-our old nature and cravings that want their way

Regardless, they are all our enemies and must bow under the power of God and His word.

2. <u>Watch out for Strongholds</u>

Strongholds are an ingrained pattern of thinking or behaving that is contrary to Jesus' words and is destructive to us. The longer you allow or validate a stronghold, the deeper the groove becomes. Each time you argue against a stronghold with the truth, you fill in that groove bit by bit.

The enemy would love to wear you down and harass you, hoping you'll give up—but don't. If he gets especially persistent, command that harassing spirit to leave you. Don't become lax concerning a stronghold, the enemy is always looking for a foothold.

2 Corinthians 10:3-5 For though we live in the world, we do not wage war as the world does. The weapons we fight with are not the weapons of the world. On the contrary, they have divine power to demolish strongholds. We demolish arguments and every pretension that sets itself up against the knowledge of God, and we take captive every thought to make it obedient to Christ. (NIV)

3. Truth: The Word of God

God's word is truth and brings faith and freedom. The only power Satan has over God's children is getting us to believe a lie. The power of God is the Truth.

Romans 10:17 Consequently, faith comes from hearing the message, and the message is heard through the word about Christ. (NIV)

2 Timothy 3:16-17 All Scripture is God-breathed and is useful for teaching, rebuking, correcting and training in righteousness, so that the servant of God may be thoroughly equipped for every good work. (NIV)

John 8:31-32 Then Jesus said to those Jews who believed Him, "If you abide in My word, you are My disciples indeed. And you shall know the truth, and the truth shall make you free." (NKJV)

John 17:17-19 (Jesus prayed) "Make them holy by your truth; teach them your word, which is truth. Just as you sent Me into the world, I am sending them into the world. And I give Myself as a holy sacrifice for them so they can be made holy by your truth." (NLT)

4. Pray with authority

As we walk in Christ, we have all power over the enemy. In the name of Jesus, we can bind the enemy and loose people from strongholds. We can resist the enemy, and he will flee.

Luke 9:1 Then He called His twelve disciples together and gave them power and authority over all demons, and to cure diseases. (NKJV)

Matthew 16:19 "I will give you the keys of the kingdom of heaven; whatever you bind on earth will be bound in heaven, and whatever you loose on earth will be loosed in heaven." (NIV)

James 4:7 Submit yourselves, then, to God. Resist the devil, and he will flee from you. (NIV)

Ephesians 6:17-18 Take the helmet of salvation and the sword of the Spirit, which is the word of God. And pray in the Spirit on all occasions with all kinds of prayers and requests. With this in mind, be alert and always keep on praying for all the Lord's people. (NIV)

5. Dart Buster: Faith

The bible refers to Satan's attacks on our spirit, mind, and emotions as *fiery darts*. In faith, hold up the words of God between you and the enemy.

Ephesians 6:16 ...above all, taking the shield of faith with which you will be able to quench all the fiery darts of the wicked one. (NKJV)

6. Pray with Others

When we become weighed down with attacks, are too tired, or are sick, we need a friend to come alongside and agree with us in prayer. Develop at least two people whom you can call to pray with you during these times.

Matthew 18:19-20 "Again, truly I tell you if two of you on earth agree about anything they ask for, it will be done for them by My Father in heaven. For where two or three gather in my name, there am I with them." (NIV)

7. Praise God for His Goodnessco

In our praise, God surrounds us with His presence which increases our faith and causes the enemy to flee.

1 Peter 2:9 ...for you are a chosen people. You are royal priests, a holy nation, God's very own possession. As a result, you can show others the goodness of God, for He called you out of the darkness into his wonderful light. (NLT)

2 Corinthians 1:3-4 Praise be to the God and Father of our Lord Jesus Christ, the Father of compassion and the God of all comfort, who comforts us in all our troubles, (NIV)

Psalm 16:7-8 I will praise the LORD, who counsels me; even at night my heart instructs me. I keep my eyes always on the LORD. With Him at my right hand, I will not be shaken. (NIV)

Become competent using the weapons God has given. They are simple but powerful. As you use the rest of this handbook, renew your mind by saturating it with the truth. Ask the Holy Spirit to dwell in you and to give you power and freedom in Christ.

CHAPTER THREE
OUR STRATEGY

Practice using these weapons whenever you battle fear, anxiety, conflict, or destructive thoughts or actions. Use discernment and ask God what lies we have believed about ourselves or others. Then find the scriptural truth in the Word that counters those lies. This is where diligence pays off and the real work begins. This is spiritual warfare.

When You Are Attacked:

1. Use Discernment

Listen and ask. What am I hearing? Whose voice is it? Mine? Someone in the world? Satan? You'll know it is the enemy if it *steals, kills, or destroys*—steals your peace, kills your love, destroys your hope, faith, relationships, etc.

Examples of things you might hear:

"You'll never be well."

"No one will ever love you."

"You always... She never..."

"See if I ever do anything around here again."

"It will feel so good, so just do it."

"You'll always be poor."

2. Classify it

Does it feel like:

-Addiction, Lust

-Anger

-Bitterness

-Complaining, Ingratitude

-Condemnation, Guilt, Shame

-Criticism, Judgmental Thoughts

-Discouragement, Hopelessness, Oppression

-Fear of Rejection, Harm, the Future

-Greed, Idolatry

-Low Self-esteem, Unworthiness

-Loneliness

-Poverty, Scarcity

-Pride

-Rebellion, Willfulness

-Resentment, Being Offended

-Unbelief

-Unforgiveness

3. Pray Truth with Authority in Faith

Now that you've discerned what is opposing you, use the verses in the Word of God which counter the enemy's lies, attacks, and strategy. Read the scriptures in the next section and pray the sample prayers. Do this as often as needed.

Align your mind and beliefs with those truths to counter the enemy's lies. Write your favorite verses on cards and keep them with you to counter the assaulting thoughts. The enemy would love to wear you down hoping you'll give up—but don't. Instead, command that harassing spirit to leave.

4. Pray with another believer

There is power in numbers!

5. Begin to Sing and Praise God

We drown out the enemy's words by singing about the love, faithfulness, and power of God and his Son, Jesus.

CHAPTER FOUR
ALIGN WITH THE TRUTH

After you have discerned what seems to be attacking you, it's time to do spiritual warfare. In everyday life, it's not so much about confronting demons as it is about banishing the lies and accusations our enemies bring.

This is where the real work begins. Listed on the following pages are some major categories of issues that keep us in bondage. Under each title are key scriptural truths to contemplate and compare against what you've been hearing or believing. Feel free to add other scriptures that you find powerful.

Example prayers are provided to say out loud. You might come up with a prayer that fits your situation even better. There is a difference between praying and warring, as I understand and have experienced. In prayer, we are asking God to help us. In warring, we are using our divine authority given by Jesus to His Body, the Church. In His name, and according to His Word, we command the thoughts and lies to leave us. We bind the power they've had over us, and we loose ourselves to be free to believe the truth.

Because God's Word *is* Truth, scriptures are more than words on a page, there is power in them—more power than we could ever have imagined.

So, it's time. Locate the thing you are having difficulty with (listed alphabetically on the following pages) and read what God has to say about it. Agree with God and resist the lies you've been believing.

Addiction, Impurity, Lust

Hebrews 2:18 Because He Himself suffered when He was tempted, He is able to help those who are being tempted. (NIV)

James 1:13-15 And remember, when you are being tempted, do not say, 'God is tempting me.' God is never tempted to do wrong, and He never tempts anyone else. Temptation comes from our own desires, which entice us and drag us away. These desires give birth to sinful actions. And when sin is allowed to grow, it gives birth to death. (NLT)

2 Corinthians 10:5 Casting down imaginations, and every high thing that exalts itself against the knowledge of God, and bringing into captivity every thought to the obedience of Christ; (KJV)

Proverbs 5:15-18 Drink water from your own cistern, running water from your own well. Should your springs overflow in the streets, your streams of water in the public squares? Let them be yours alone, never to be shared with strangers. May your fountain be blessed, and may you rejoice in the wife of your youth. (NIV)

Galatians 6:7-8 Do not be deceived: God cannot be mocked. A man reaps what he sows. Whoever sows to please their flesh, from the flesh will reap destruction; whoever sows to please the Spirit, from the Spirit will reap eternal life. (NIV)

Ezekiel 36:26 And I will give you a new heart, and I will put a new spirit in you. I will take out your stony, stubborn heart and give you a tender, responsive heart. (NLT)

1 John 5:4 …for everyone born of God overcomes the world. This is the victory that has overcome the world, even our faith. (NIV)

Hebrews 10:14 For by one offering He forever made perfect those who are being made holy. (NLT)

2 Corinthians 5:17 Therefore, if anyone is in Christ, he is a new creation; old things have passed away; behold, all things have become new. (NKJV)

Philippians 1:6 …being confident of this, that He who began a good work in you will carry it on to completion until the day of Christ Jesus. (NIV)

Philippians 4:8 Finally, brothers and sisters, whatever is true, whatever is noble, whatever is right, whatever is pure, whatever is lovely, whatever is admirable—if anything is excellent or praiseworthy—think about such things. (NIV)

EXAMPLE PRAYER:

"You destructive spirit of lust and addiction, I bind your power over me now in the name of Jesus Christ. I forbid you to speak to me and I cast you out of my mind, body, emotions and spirit. By the authority given to me by Jesus Christ, I forbid you to operate in my life.

Lord, I denounce the impurity in my heart. I know my natural heart is deceitful above all things and desperately wicked. Thank You for taking this wicked heart and exchanging it for a pure heart that refuses to entertain evil. I declare I am a new creation in Christ, my old life is gone, and all things have become new. Help keep my mind pure and filled with righteous thoughts of good, honest, noble, lovely, and virtuous things.

I know You are transforming me into your image, that temptation is not sin, and that You don't condemn me. In fact, You already see me as perfect, even while I am being transformed.

Help me to use Your weapons to bring every thought captive to the obedience of Christ. Help me to flee from temptation. I praise you for your faithfulness, and I trust in You alone!"

Anger

Proverbs 22:24-25 Don't befriend angry people or associate with hot-tempered people, or you will learn to be like them and endanger your soul. (NLT)

Proverbs 29:22-23 An angry person stirs up conflict, and a hot-tempered person commits many sins. Pride brings a person low, but the lowly in spirit gain honor. (NIV)

Ecclesiastes 7:9 Do not be quickly provoked in your spirit, for anger resides in the lap of fools. (NIV)

Ephesians 4:26-27,31,32 In your anger do not sin: Do not let the sun go down while you are still angry, and do not give the devil a foothold. Get rid of all bitterness, rage and anger, brawling and slander, along with every form of malice. Be kind and compassionate to one another, forgiving each other just as in Christ, God forgave you. (NIV)

Colossians 3:7-8 You used to walk in these ways, in the life you once lived. But now you must rid yourselves of all such things as these: anger, rage, malice, slander, and filthy language from your lips. (NIV)

James 1:19-20 My dear brothers, take note of this: Everyone should be quick to listen, slow to speak and slow to become angry, for man's anger does not bring about the righteous life that God desires. Therefore, get rid of all moral filth and the evil that is so prevalent, and humbly accept the word planted in you, which can save you. (NIV)

Psalm 37:7-9, 12 -13, 15 Be still before the Lord and wait patiently for Him; do not fret when people succeed in their ways, when they carry out their wicked schemes. Refrain from anger and turn from wrath; do not fret—it leads only to evil. For those who are evil will be destroyed, but those who hope in the Lord will inherit the land. (NIV)

The whole of **Psalm 37** gives us power over those who have hurt us. We can even afford compassion toward them when we realize their end.

EXAMPLE PRAYER:

"You angry spirit, according to the Word of God, I bind you now in the name of Jesus Christ. I forbid you to speak to me and cast you out of my mind, body, emotions and spirit.

Lord, I know that my anger can never achieve Your righteousness, and that You will reckon with those who have hurt me. I pray for those who are hurtful, that they may repent and be saved from their wickedness. Help me not to be hurtful in retaliation.

Holy Spirit, live in me and cause me to live in You fully. Exchange my anger for Your love, joy, peace, longsuffering, kindness, goodness, gentleness, and self-control. I know I can do all things through Christ who strengthens me. Thank You for changing me right now by the power of Your Spirit!"

Bitterness

Ephesians 4:30-32 And do not bring sorrow to God's Holy Spirit by the way you live. Remember, He has identified you as His own, guaranteeing that you will be saved on the day of redemption. Get rid of all bitterness, rage, anger, harsh words, and slander, as well as all types of evil behavior. Instead, be kind to each other, tenderhearted, forgiving one another, just as God through Christ has forgiven you. (NLT)

Hebrews 12:14-15 Make every effort to live in peace with everyone and to be holy; without holiness no one will see the Lord. See to it that no one falls short of the grace of God and that no bitter root grows up to cause trouble and defile many. (NIV)

EXAMPLE PRAYER:

"Father, I forsake all bitterness that has been in my life. I know that when I allow bitterness to spring up within me, it acts as a root and brings forth all kinds of evil. It tortures my soul and robs me of joy and peace. Since you commanded me to put away bitterness, it must be a matter of choice for me. I choose to let go of it and not hold onto it as my 'due' for the wrongs done to me. I know it only poisons my soul and those around me.

In Jesus' name, and by the power that raised Him from the dead, I release my bitterness and choose to pursue peace with all people. Help me, Holy Spirit to resist this temptation and think higher thoughts that work *for* me and *for* my relationships. Bless You Lord for setting me free!"

Complaining, Ingratitude

Philippians 2:14-15 Do everything without complaining and arguing, so that no one can criticize you. Live clean, innocent lives as children of God, shining like bright lights in a world full of crooked and perverse people. (NLT)

1 Peter 4:9 Be hospitable to one another without grumbling. (NKJV)

Deuteronomy 1:34 When the Lord heard your complaining, He became very angry. (NLT)

Ephesians 4:29 Don't use foul or abusive language. Let everything you say be good and helpful, so that your words will be an encouragement to those who hear them. (NLT)

Psalm 147:7 Sing to the Lord with grateful praise; make music to our God on the harp. (NIV)

Psalm 23:6 Surely goodness and mercy shall follow me All the days of my life; And I will dwell in the house of the Lord Forever. (NKJV)

Psalm 31:19 Oh, how great is Your goodness, Which You have laid up for those who fear You, Which You have prepared for those who trust in You in the presence of the sons of men! (NKJV)

Psalm 107:8 Oh, that men would give thanks to the Lord for His goodness, And for His wonderful works to the children of men! (NKJV)

EXAMPLE PRAYER:

"Father God, I didn't realize how much You hate hearing your children complain. I am sorry I've wasted so much of my breath grumbling and complaining. I want to stop. Instead, help me release words of encouragement to those around me.

I rebuke a spirit of ingratitude in my heart right now and the stronghold it has had on me. I ask You Lord to replace it with a spirit of joy and praise. You have done so much for me. Help me focus on Your goodness and the everlasting life that waits for me!

Condemnation, Guilt, Shame

John 3:17-18 "For God did not send his Son into the world to condemn the world, but to save the world through Him. Whoever believes in Him is not condemned..." (NIV)

Romans 8:1 Therefore, there is now no condemnation for those who are in Christ Jesus... (NIV)

1 John 1:9 If we confess our sins, He is faithful and just and will forgive us our sins and purify us from all unrighteousness. (NIV)

Revelation 12:10 It has come at last — salvation and power and the Kingdom of our God, and the authority of His Christ. For the accuser of our brothers and sisters has been thrown down to earth — the one who accuses them before our God day and night. (NLT)

EXAMPLE PRAYER:

"You condemning spirit, leave me now in the name of Jesus. The Word of God tells me there is no condemnation to those who are in Christ Jesus, and I am in Christ Jesus. I forbid you to accuse me anymore. I have confessed my sins before God and am forgiven by the blood of Jesus Christ. He has cleansed me from all unrighteousness. He began a good work in me and is faithful to finish that work. I will be transformed into the image of Jesus Christ!

You condemning spirit, I reject the accusing thoughts you bring to my mind against other people. I resist the temptation to accuse, blame, and belittle others in my mind or my words.

Christ, you died for them. You love them and are patient as You transform them. Thank You for helping me to pray for them, to be compassionate, and to love the way You do! I love this freedom!"

Critical, Judgmental Thoughts

Matthew 7:3-5 "Why do you look at the speck of sawdust in your brother's eye and pay no attention to the plank in your own eye? How can you say to your brother, 'Let me take the speck out of your eye,' when all the time there is a plank in your own eye? You hypocrite, first take the plank out of your own eye, and then you will see clearly to remove the speck from your brother's eye." (NIV)

Romans 2:1-6 You, therefore, have no excuse, you who pass judgment on someone else, for at whatever point you judge another, you are condemning yourself, because you who pass judgment do the same things. Now we know that God's judgment against those who do such things is based on truth. So when you, a mere human being, pass judgment on them and yet do the same things, do you think you will escape God's judgment? Or do you show contempt for the riches of His kindness, forbearance and patience, not realizing that God's kindness is intended to lead you to repentance? (NIV)

Romans 14:13 So let's stop condemning each other. Decide instead to live in such a way that you will not cause another believer to stumble and fall. (NLT)

James 2:13 ...judgment without mercy will be shown to anyone who has not been merciful. Mercy triumphs over judgment! (NIV)

Galatians 5:14-15 For the entire law is fulfilled in keeping this one command: "Love your neighbor as yourself." If you bite and devour each other, watch out or you will be destroyed by each other. (NIV)

EXAMPLE PRAYER:

"You critical spirit, according to the Word of God, I bind you now in the name of Jesus Christ. I forbid you to speak to me and cast you out of my mind, body, emotions and spirit.

Lord, I ask forgiveness for giving in to a critical spirit and for judging others. You alone are holy enough to make a righteous judgment. I choose to show mercy, because I also need mercy. Cleanse my mind from these thought patterns that have dug in deeply. Fill me with Your love which covers a multitude of sins. Help me to focus on the good in people rather than their shortcomings.

And Lord, help me to look at the good that You are creating in me and not on the imperfections. If You do not judge me, and criticize me, who am I to be harsh with myself? I confess that it is a sin for me to be critical of Your servants, including myself. Therefore, I know to do good, and I will not sin against you by being critical. I can do all things through Christ who strengthens me!"

Discouragement, Hopelessness, Oppression

Isaiah 41:10 So do not fear, for I am with you; do not be dismayed, for I am your God. I will strengthen you and help you; I will uphold you with My righteous right hand. (NIV)

Nehemiah 8:10 Do not grieve, for the joy of the Lord is your strength. (NIV)

Deuteronomy 31:6, 8 Be strong and courageous. Do not be afraid or terrified because of them, for the Lord your God goes with you; He will never leave you nor forsake you. The Lord Himself goes before you and will be with you; He will never leave you nor forsake you. Do not be afraid; do not be discouraged. (NIV)

Psalm 30:5 Weeping may endure for a night, but joy comes in the morning. (NKJV)

Psalm 107:26-31 They mounted up to the heavens and went down to the depths; in their peril their courage melted away. They reeled and staggered like drunken men; they were at their wits' end. Then they cried out to the Lord in their trouble, and He brought them out of their distress. He stilled the storm to a whisper; the waves of the sea were hushed. They were glad when it grew calm, and He guided them to their desired haven. Let them give thanks to the Lord for His unfailing love and His wonderful deeds for men. (NIV)

Philippians 1:6 ...being confident of this, that He who began a good work in you will carry it on to completion until the day of Christ Jesus. (NIV)

Hebrews 12:2 ...looking unto Jesus, the author and finisher of our faith, who for the joy that was set before Him endured the cross, despising the shame, and has sat down at the right hand of the throne of God. (NKJV)

Jerimiah 29:11 "For I know the plans I have for you," declares the Lord, "plans to prosper you and not to harm you, plans to give you hope and a future." (NIV)

EXAMPLE PRAYER:

"You oppressive spirit of discouragement and hopelessness, I bind your power over me now in the name of Jesus Christ. I forbid you to speak to me and cast you out of my mind, body, emotions and spirit. By the authority given to me by Jesus Christ, I forbid you to operate in my life.

Father, I am so encouraged by Your Word. I will saturate my mind with Your Word. I already have the victory because I walk in Your strength, not my own. I am born of God and already possess a measure of faith, which You are increasing. You have a good plan for my life. Lift me up this day and put Your song in my heart. I know that the joy of the Lord is my strength. My hope is in Jesus alone. Thank you for hearing me and loving me today!"

Fear of Rejection, Harm, the Future

Philippians 4:6-7 Do not be anxious about anything, but in every situation, by prayer and petition, with thanksgiving, present your requests to God. And the peace of God, which transcends all understanding, will guard your hearts and your minds in Christ Jesus. (NIV)

Psalm 23:4 Yes, though I walk in the valley of the shadow of death, I will fear no evil, for You are with me; Your rod and staff, they comfort me. (NKJV)

Psalm 56:3-4 When I am afraid, I put my trust in You. In God, whose word I praise—in God I trust and am not afraid. What can mere mortals do to me? (NIV)

Isaiah 41:10 So do not fear, for I am with you; do not be dismayed, for I am your God. I will strengthen you and help you; I will uphold you with My righteous right hand. (NIV)

Isaiah 54:17 ...no weapon forged against you will prevail, and you will refute every tongue that accuses you. This is the heritage of the servants of the Lord... (NIV)

2 Timothy 1:7 For God has not given us a spirit of fear, but of power, and of love, and of a sound mind. (NKJV)

EXAMPLE PRAYER:

"You lying, deceiving spirit of fear, I command you to leave me in the name of Jesus. I forbid you to speak to me and cast you out of my mind, body, emotions and spirit. By the authority given to me by Jesus Christ, I forbid you to operate in my life.

I declare that God has not given me the spirit of fear, but of love and power and a sound mind. I will not fear because God is with me. The angel of the Lord encamps all around me and delivers me. I thank God that no weapon formed against me shall prosper. Holy Spirit, come and fill my mind with the truth that if God is for me, no one can be against me. Help me know there is a way out of my difficulty that I haven't seen yet. Please, show me the path to take. I trust YOU!"

Greed, Idolatry

Luke 12:15 Then He said, "Beware! Guard against every kind of greed. Life is not measured by how much you own." (NLT)

Ephesians 5:5 For of this you can be sure: No immoral, impure or greedy person—such a person is an idolater—has any inheritance in the kingdom of Christ and of God. (NIV)

Colossians 3:5 Put to death, therefore, whatever belongs to your earthly nature: sexual immorality, impurity, lust, evil desires and greed, which is idolatry. (NIV)

1 Corinthians 13-14 No temptation has overtaken you except such as is common to man; but God is faithful, who will not allow you to be tempted beyond what you are able, but with the temptation will also make the way of escape, that you may be able to bear it. Therefore, my beloved, flee from idolatry. (NKJV)

Matthew 6:31-33 "So don't worry about these things, saying, 'What will we eat? What will we drink? What will we wear?' These things dominate the thoughts of unbelievers, but your heavenly Father already knows all your needs. But seek first His kingdom and His righteousness, and all these things will be given to you as well." (NIV)

1 Timothy 6:6 But godliness with contentment is great gain. (NKJV)

EXAMPLE PRAYER:

"Father, I see I have been consumed by greed, wanting more and never being content. I have made this world's riches an idol, constantly pursuing material things instead of pursuing You and Your kingdom with all my heart. This has caused strife and anxiety, has taken my peace, and broken my close relationship with You. Please forgive me and break the hold this has had over my life.

In Jesus' name, I cast out all greed and idolatry. I choose the riches of contentment, a clean heart, and a right spirit. Father, I know You desire to bless Your children with good things but help me discern when something is tempting me to the point of greed or idolatry. I am filled with great joy knowing you are delivering me from striving and are working contentment and joy into my life!"

Low Self-esteem, Unworthiness

Psalm 139:1-6 O Lord, you have examined my heart and know everything about me. You know when I sit down or stand up. You know my thoughts even when I'm far away. You see me when I travel and when I rest at home. You know everything I do. You know what I am going to say even before I say it, Lord. You go before me and follow me. You place your hand of blessing on my head. Such knowledge is too wonderful for me, too great for me to understand! (NLT)

Psalm 139:14-16 I praise you because I am fearfully and wonderfully made; Your works are wonderful, I know that full well. My frame was not hidden from You when I was made in the secret place. When I was woven together in the depths of the earth, Your eyes saw my unformed body. All the days ordained for me were written in Your book before one of them came to be. (NIV)

Song of Solomon 4:7 You are altogether beautiful, my darling; there is no flaw in you. (NIV)

1 Corinthians 6:11 And that is what some of you were. But you were washed, you were sanctified, you were justified in the name of the Lord Jesus Christ and by the Spirit of our God. (NIV)

2 Corinthians 5:17 Therefore, if anyone is in Christ, he is a new creation; old things have passed away; behold, all things have become new. (NKJV)

Philippians 1:6 ...being confident of this, that He who began a good work in you will carry it on to completion until the day of Christ Jesus. (NIV)

John 15:9 "As the Father has loved me, so have I loved you. Now remain in my love." (NIV)

Romans 8:38-39 For I am persuaded that neither death nor life, nor angels nor principalities nor powers, nor things present nor things to come, nor height nor depth, nor any other created thing, shall be able to separate us from the love of God which is in Christ Jesus our Lord. (NKJV)

EXAMPLE PRAYER:

"You spirit of unworthiness, by the authority given to me by Jesus Christ, I bind you and forbid you to speak to me. I cast you out of my mind, body, emotions, and spirit and I forbid you to operate in my life.

I am a beautiful new creation in Christ. The old things of my life have passed away and everything has become new. I declare I am wonderfully made by my God. He fashioned all my days and thinks of me constantly. His thoughts towards me are for peace and not for evil. He has promised to perfect me into the image of Jesus Christ, and I believe Him. Holy Spirit, help me to keep believing what God says about me. Thank you, Lord!"

Loneliness

Psalm 107:9 For He satisfies the longing soul and fills the hungry soul with goodness. (NKJV)

Psalm 139:1-6 O Lord, you have examined my heart and know everything about me. You know when I sit down or stand up. You know my thoughts even when I'm far away. You see me when I travel and when I rest at home. You know everything I do. You know what I am going to say even before I say it, Lord. You go before me and follow me. You place Your hand of blessing on my head. Such knowledge is too wonderful for me, too great for me to understand! (NLT)

Psalm 139:7-10 Where can I go from Your Spirit? Where can I flee from Your presence? If I go up to the heavens, You are there; if I make my bed in the depths, You are there. If I rise on the wings of the dawn, if I settle on the far side of the sea, even there Your hand will guide me, Your right hand will hold me fast. (NIV)

Psalm 139:17-18 How precious to me are Your thoughts, O God! How vast is the sum of them! Were I to count them, they would outnumber the grains of sand. When I awake, I am still with You. (NIV)

Matthew 28:20 "And surely I am with you always, to the very end of the age." (NIV)

James 4:8 Come close to God, and God will come close to you. (NLT)

EXAMPLE PRAYER:

"Lord, I have believed a lie that I am alone. Your word tells me that You are with me constantly. Your thoughts toward me are as numerous as the sands of the oceans. Help me to know You more and draw closer to You. For You are my comforter and my help when I am in need.

Lord, help me not to dwell on my situation, but to look for ways to serve You. Holy Spirit, come and comfort me now and help me to comfort others with the same comfort I have received. You are with me even now!"

Poverty, Scarcity

Matthew 6:31-33 "So don't worry about these things, saying, 'What will we eat? What will we drink? What will we wear?' These things dominate the thoughts of unbelievers, but your heavenly Father already knows all your needs. Seek the Kingdom of God above all else, and live righteously, and He will give you everything you need." (NLT)

Luke 6:37-39 "Give, and you will receive. Your gift will return to you in full — pressed down, shaken together to make room for more, running over, and poured into your lap. The amount you give will determine the amount you get back." (NLT)

Malachi 3:10-12 "Bring all the tithes into the storehouse, that there may be food in My house, and try Me now in this," Says the Lord of hosts, "If I will not open for you the windows of heaven and pour out for you such blessing that there will not be room enough to receive it. And I will rebuke the devourer for your sakes, so that he will not destroy the fruit of your ground, nor shall the vine fail to bear fruit for you in the field," says the Lord of hosts; (NKJV)

Acts 10:30-31 So Cornelius said, "Four days ago I was fasting until this hour; and at the ninth hour I prayed in my house, and behold, a man stood before me in bright clothing, and said, 'Cornelius, your prayer has been heard, and your alms are remembered in the sight of God. ... (NKJV)

Proverbs 11:25 A generous person will prosper; whoever refreshes others will be refreshed. (NIV)

EXAMPLE PRAYER:

"Lord, as I look at my life, all I see is scarcity and poverty, never enough to meet my needs no matter how hard I try. I see I have been operating under the world's strategy of trying to get everything I can. Now I see that you have a better and opposite strategy for abundance: to give away first, and then You will bless what I have left.

This takes more faith than I've ever had, so please, strengthen my faith in Your promises. Help me to give a tithe to You. Help me see ways I can give to others to meet their needs, and know You are faithful to do what You say. Help me learn to live as generously as I can.

I claim Your promises as I walk in obedience, that You will bless me more than I can ever give away. Thank You for taking me on this next step in my faith journey with You!"

Pride

Psalm 10:4 The wicked are too proud to seek God. They seem to think that God is dead. (NLT)

Proverbs 6:16-19 These six things the Lord hates, yes, seven are an abomination to Him: a proud look, a lying tongue, and hands that shed innocent blood, a heart that devises wicked plans, feet that are swift in running to evil. A false witness who speaks lies, and one who sows discord among brethren. (NKJV)

Proverbs 8:13 To fear the Lord is to hate evil; I hate pride and arrogance, evil behavior, and perverse speech. (NIV)

Proverbs 16:18 Pride goes before destruction, a haughty spirit before a fall. (NIV)

Romans 12:3 Do not think of yourself more highly than you ought, but rather think of yourself with sober judgment, (NIV)

Matthew 23:12 For those who exalt themselves will be humbled, and those who humble themselves will be exalted. (NIV)

James 4:6-7 God resists the proud but gives grace to the humble. Therefore, submit to God. Resist the devil and he will flee from you. (NKJV)

James 4:10 Humble yourselves before the Lord, and He will lift you up (NIV)

Proverbs 22:4 The reward of humility and the fear of the Lord are riches, honor, and life. (NASB)

EXAMPLE PRAYER:

"Father, in the name of Jesus, I come against this prideful spirit that has ruled my life. I bind its power over me and forbid it to operate in my life.

I confess that I have sought to glorify myself instead of You. Please replace this false pride with a spirit of thankfulness for the way You have made me and the things You have given to me. Help me to humble myself in Your sight and not to think more highly of myself than I should.

If I need to be loved or validated, help me to receive those things from You instead of acting prideful or trying to excel to win the praise of man. You are able to heal my feelings of inadequacy and to give me a thankful and humble heart. I rejoice that I can find my strength and confidence in You!"

Rebellion, Willfulness

1 Samuel 15:23 For rebellion is as the sin of witchcraft, and stubbornness is as iniquity and idolatry. (NKJV)

Isaiah 30:9 For these are rebellious people, deceitful children, children unwilling to listen to the Lord's instruction. (NIV)

Proverbs 5:11-13 In the end you will groan in anguish when disease consumes your body. You will say, "How I hated discipline! If only I had not ignored all the warnings! Oh, why didn't I listen to my teachers? ... Why didn't I pay attention to my instructors?" (NLT)

Psalm 68:6 God sets the lonely in families, He leads forth the prisoners with singing; but the rebellious live in a sun-scorched land. (NIV)

Psalm 107:17 Some became fools through their rebellious ways and suffered affliction because of their iniquities. (NIV)

Isaiah 1:19-20 If you are willing and obedient, you shall eat the good of the land; But if you refuse and rebel, you shall be devoured by the sword; (NKJV)

Hebrews 3:7-13 That is why the Holy Spirit says, "Today, if you hear His voice, do not harden your hearts as you did in the rebellion, during the time of testing in the desert, where your fathers tested and tried Me and for forty years saw what I did." That is why I was angry with that generation, and I said, "Their hearts are always going astray, and they have not known My ways." So I declared on oath in my anger, "They shall never enter My rest." See to it, brothers, that none of you has a sinful, unbelieving heart that turns away from the living God. But encourage one another daily, as long as it is called Today, so that none of you may be hardened by sin's deceitfulness. (NIV)

Ezekiel 36:26 "I will give you a new heart and put a new spirit within you; I will take the heart of stone out of your flesh and give you a heart of flesh." (NKJV)

Philippians 4:13 I can do all things through Christ who strengthens me. (NKJV)

Revelation 21:3-4 And I heard a loud voice from the throne saying, "Look! God's dwelling place is now among the people, and he will dwell with them. They will be his people, and God himself will be with them and be their God. He will wipe every tear from their eyes. There will be no more death or mourning or crying or pain, for the old order of things has passed away." (NIV)

EXAMPLE PRAYER:

"You wicked spirit of rebellion, I bind you and cast you out of my life in the name of Jesus. I renounce every rebellious thought as it comes to me. I forbid you to operate in my life.

Lord, I confess that I have had a rebellious spirit. I have exalted myself and my own way above Your commandments and have not submitted my will to You. I see the price I pay as I push and strive for my own way. I give up.

Help me to trust You and Your good path for my life. Help me discern when I am being rebellious. Help me listen to instruction and obey Your Word. I know You are giving me the will and the power to do what pleases You. Thank You for being my God and preparing an eternal heaven for me!"

Resentment, Being Offended

2 Timothy 2:24-26 And the Lord's servant must not be quarrelsome, but must be kind to everyone, able to teach, not resentful. Opponents must be gently instructed, in the hope that God will grant them repentance leading them to a knowledge of the truth, and that they will come to their senses and escape from the trap of the devil, who has taken them captive to do his will. (NIV)

Matthew 5:44-48 "But I tell you, love your enemies and pray for those who persecute you, that you may be children of your Father in heaven. He causes His sun to rise on the evil and the good and sends rain on the righteous and the unrighteous. If you love those who love you, what reward will you get? Are not even the tax collectors doing that? And if you greet only your own people, what are you doing more than others? Do not even pagans do that? Be perfect, therefore, as your heavenly Father is perfect." (NIV)

Proverbs 3:11-12 My son, do not despise the chastening of the Lord, nor detest His correction; for whom the Lord loves He corrects, just as a father the son in whom he delights. (NKJV)

Proverbs 19:11 Sensible people control their temper; they earn respect by overlooking wrongs. (NLT)

Galatians 6:9 So let's not get tired of doing what is good. At just the right time we will reap a harvest of blessing if we don't give up. (NLT)

EXAMPLE PRAYER:

"You spirit of resentment, I bind you and cast you out of my life in the name of Jesus. I resist the temptation to be offended and renounce every resentful thought that comes to me. By the authority given to me by Jesus Christ, I forbid you to operate in my life.

Lord, I have resented people and circumstances that have come into my life. It seems that the people I have loved and trusted the most have hurt me the most, including my Christian brothers and sisters. Help me to forgive them for the pain and frustration they have caused me. Give me the patience I need to live with imperfect people and in this imperfect world.

Help me to see that I've also offended others and need their forgiveness and patience. I know it takes more love and power than I have to act differently from the way unbelievers do, to love people with Your unconditional love. Please, give me that desire and power in my heart and mind. Help me to trust that all of these circumstances will create a Godly character in me and cause me to shine like pure gold!"

Unbelief

Hebrews 3:12 Be careful then, dear brothers and sisters. Make sure that your own hearts are not evil and unbelieving, turning you away from the living God. (NLT)

Romans 14:23 ...for whatever is not from faith is sin. (NKJV)

Luke 12:29-31 "And do not set your heart on what you will eat or drink; do not worry about it. For the pagan world runs after all such things, and your Father knows that you need them. But seek His kingdom, and these things will be given to you as well." (NIV)

Romans 4:18, 20, 21 Against all hope, Abraham in hope believed and so became the father of many nations, ...he did not waver through unbelief regarding the promise of God but was strengthened in his faith and gave glory to God, being fully persuaded that God had power to do what He had promised. (NIV)

Hebrews 11:1 Now faith is the substance of things hoped for, the evidence of things not seen. (NKJV)

2 Timothy 1:12 ...I am suffering...Yet this is no cause for shame, because I know whom I have believed and am convinced that He is able to guard what I have entrusted to Him for that day. (NIV)

Mark 9:23-24 Jesus said to him, "If you can believe, all things are possible to him who believes." Immediately the father of the child cried out and said with tears, "Lord, I believe; help my unbelief!" (NKJV)

Matthew 7:7 "Ask, and it will be given to you; seek, and you will find; knock, and it will be opened to you." (NIV)

EXAMPLE PRAYER:

"You deceitful spirit of unbelief, I bind you in the name of Jesus. I have allowed you to poison my mind with unbelief which is sin. By the authority of Jesus Christ, I forbid you to operate in my life.

Father God, you are trustworthy and able to do exceedingly abundantly above all I can ask or think. You say that all things work together for my good, therefore, I choose to believe even when things don't go the way I planned. Lord, when I am weak, help my unbelief. Help me to be like the tree that is planted by the water, with strong roots of faith so I can shout, 'I shall not be moved!'"

Unforgiveness

Matthew 6:12-15 "Pray...Forgive us our debts, as we also have forgiven our debtors. And lead us not into temptation but deliver us from the evil one. For if you forgive other people when they sin against you, your heavenly Father will also forgive you. But if you do not forgive others their sins, your Father will not forgive your sins." (NIV)

Mark 11:25-27 "And whenever you stand praying, if you have anything against anyone, forgive him, that your Father in heaven may also forgive you your trespasses. But if you do not forgive, neither will your Father in heaven forgive your trespasses." (NKJV)

Matthew 18:32-35 "Then the master called the servant in. 'You wicked servant,' he said, 'I canceled all that debt of yours because you begged me to. Shouldn't you have had mercy on your fellow servant just as I had on you?' In anger his master turned him over to the jailers to be tortured, until he should pay back all he owed. This is how my heavenly Father will treat each of you unless you forgive your brother from your heart." (NIV)

(NOTE: We are also tormented internally when we hold on to unforgiveness.)

Matthew 5:7 "Blessed are the merciful, for they shall obtain mercy." (NKJV)

Luke 17:3-4 "Take heed to yourselves. If your brother sins against you, rebuke him; and if he repents, forgive him. And if he sins against you seven times in a day, and seven times in a day returns to you, saying, 'I repent,' you shall forgive him." (NKJV)

Romans 12:14, 17, 18 Bless those who persecute you; bless and do not curse...Do not repay anyone evil for evil...If it is possible, as far as it depends on you, live at peace with everyone. (NIV)

Ephesians 4:32 Be kind and compassionate to one another, forgiving each other, just as in Christ God forgave you. (NIV)

Colossians 3:13 Bear with each other and forgive one another if any of you has a grievance against someone. Forgive as the Lord forgave you. (NIV)

EXAMPLE PRAYER:

"You wicked spirit of unforgiveness, I refuse to listen to your accusations and instead choose God's wise counsel that will set me free from torment. By the authority Christ has given me, I forbid you to operate in my life.

Father, I see that forgiveness is a command, not a choice. You have forgiven me for much more than what anyone could ever do to me. I need Your forgiveness and mercy, therefore, I need to give forgiveness and show mercy. I bow my will to Yours.

I trust that You will judge my enemies rightly, and that You will bless me for my obedience to Your will. I can't do this in my own strength, so please, Father, exchange the hardness in my heart for a pure heart that chooses to please You. Set me free from this burden of unforgiveness that robs my peace and causes me to be bound up and tied to those whom I haven't forgiven.

I understand that forgiveness is for my benefit and will set me free!"

FINAL NOTE

As believers, we are called to give up our right to think and behave as unbelievers do. We are new creations—sons and daughters of God Almighty! Grasp hold of the freedom that God prepared for you. Joyfully walk in the light—for your own good and so others may see His goodness.

Although we are engaged in spiritual warfare, our battles are small in comparison to the battle Jesus won for our souls. For the joy that was set before Him, Jesus endured the cross and is now glorified and seated at the right hand of God the Father. Our battles will seem as nothing when we enter heaven and finally see Jesus, our Savior and King!

Note: If more in-depth warfare is needed, I highly recommend Neil T. Anderson's books on spiritual warfare.

Don't miss out!

Visit the website below and you can sign up to receive emails whenever Cheryl Colwell publishes a new book. There's no charge and no obligation.

https://books2read.com/r/B-A-GHOI-WCXHC

BOOKS 2 READ

Connecting independent readers to independent writers.

Also by Cheryl Colwell

The Get Eaven Series
Astoria Rumors

The Secrets of the Montebellis Series
The Secrets of the Montebellis
Adriana's Secrets

Standalone
The Proof
The Land Lord
Warring in the Spirit: Power for Everyday Living

Watch for more at www.cherylcolwell.com.

About the Author

Cheryl Colwell writes and publishes Christian fiction but has stepped into the non-fiction world to deliver a booklet she finds invaluable for Christian living. As a longtime believer in Jesus Christ, Colwell faces the common struggles of living in the world without succumbing to the world's views and habits. Re-discovering the authority given to each believer and how to pray effectively has enabled her to experience more victories than defeats. Though many books on spiritual warfare exist, she felt compelled to assemble a concise booklet for quick reference during times of struggle.

Read more at www.cherylcolwell.com.

www.ingramcontent.com/pod-product-compliance
Lightning Source LLC
Chambersburg PA
CBHW071849020426
42331CB00007B/1923